Rain

Andrea Rivera

abdopublishing.com

Published by Abdo Zoom™, PO Box 398166, Minneapolis, Minnesota 55439. Copyright © 2017 by
Abdo Consulting Group, Inc. International copyrights reserved in all countries. No part of this book may be
reproduced in any form without written permission from the publisher. Abdo Zoom™ is a trademark and logo
of Abdo Consulting Group, Inc.

Printed in the United States of America, North Mankato, Minnesota
102016
012017

 THIS BOOK CONTAINS
RECYCLED MATERIALS

Cover Photo: Shutterstock Images
Interior Photos: Shutterstock Images, 1, 8–9, 9; Brian A. Jackson/iStockphoto, 4; Pete's Photography/iStockphoto,
5; Fernando Podolski/iStockphoto, 6–7; iStockphoto, 11, 12, 19, 21; Emily Churchill/iStockphoto, 13; Rainworks,
14; Pelageya Klubnikina/iStockphoto, 16–17; Alena Ozerova/Shutterstock Images, 17; Andreas Poertner/
Shutterstock Images, 18

Editor: Emily Temple
Series Designer: Madeline Berger
Art Direction: Dorothy Toth

Publisher's Cataloging-in-Publication Data
Names: Rivera, Andrea, author.
Title: Rain / by Andrea Rivera.
Description: Minneapolis, MN : Abdo Zoom, 2017. | Series: In the sky |
    Includes bibliographical references and index.
Identifiers: LCCN 2016948920 | ISBN 9781680799330 (lib. bdg.) |
    ISBN 9781624025198 (ebook) | ISBN 9781624025754 (Read-to-me ebook)
Subjects: LCSH: Rain--Juvenile literature.
Classification: DDC 551.57/7--dc23
LC record available at http://lccn.loc.gov/2016948920

Table of Contents

Science 4

Technology. 8

Engineering 12

Art 14

Math 16

Key Stats. 20

Glossary 22

Booklinks 23

Index 24

Rain is water
that falls from clouds.

Tiny water droplets are inside a cloud. They bump into each other. They combine.

The droplets get bigger.
They get heavier.

When they get too heavy to float, they fall to the ground as rain.

Technology

Scientists try to **predict** rain. They study clouds and wind.

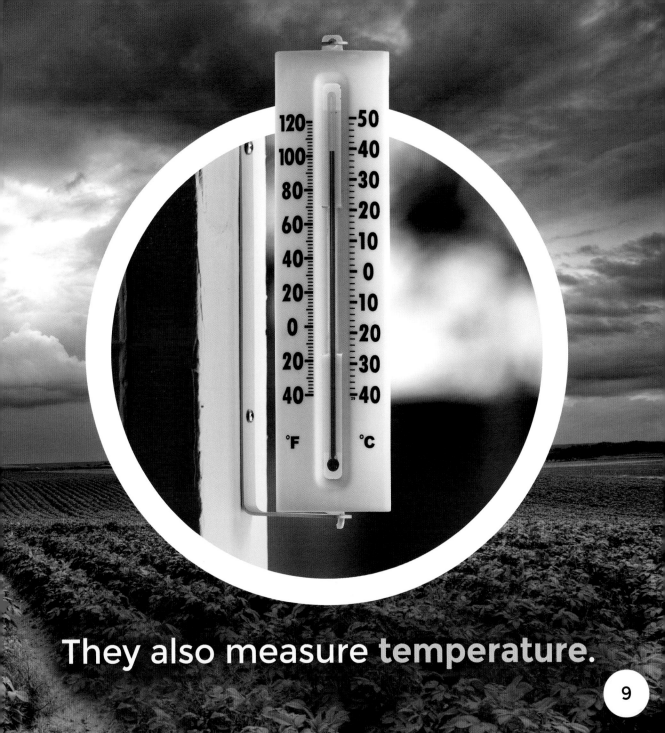

They also measure temperature.

The information goes into computer models. The models help predict the weather.

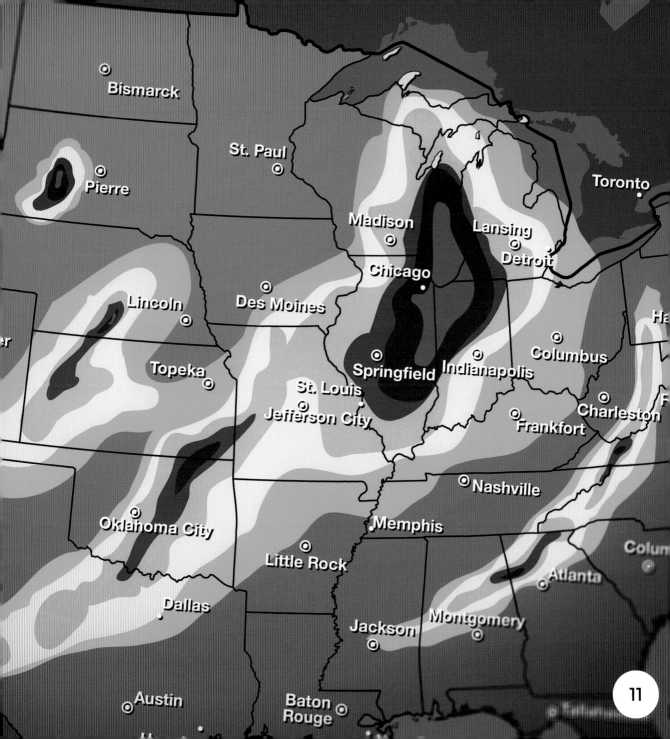

Rain jackets use waterproof fabric.

It has layers. One layer keeps out water. Another has tiny holes. The holes let the person's sweat escape. But they do not let water in.

Art

EXPLORE

Some art is only seen when it rains. Artists make pictures on roads or sidewalks.

Rain gets the
pavement wet.
It turns dark.
The pictures do not.
They stay dry.

Math

Rain is measured by how much falls in one hour. Up to 0.10 inches (0.25 cm) in one hour is light rain.

More than 0.30 inches (0.76 cm) is heavy rain.

Gauges are used to measure rain.

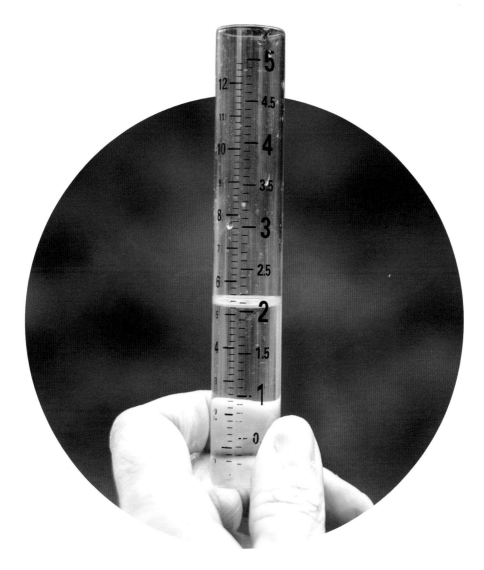

- Most raindrops are about 0.08 inches (0.2 cm) across. But they can be different sizes. Some are as big as 0.25 inches (0.6 cm) across.

- The smallest raindrops are round. Bigger raindrops get flatter.

- Freezing rain is super cold. These raindrops freeze as soon as they hit the ground. They cover things in ice.

Glossary

gauge – a tool that collects water so it can be measured.

model – a program that analyzes information and predicts what might happen.

predict - to guess what might happen in the future.

temperature - how hot or cold something is, usually measured by a thermometer.

waterproof - something that keeps out water or does not get wet.

Booklinks

For more information
on rain, please visit
booklinks.abdopublishing.com

Learn even more with the Abdo Zoom
STEAM database. Check out
abdozoom.com for more information.

Index

clouds, 4, 5, 8

computer, 10

droplets, 5, 6

fabric, 12

pictures, 14, 15

rain jackets, 12

scientists, 8

temperature, 9

water, 4, 5, 13

weather, 10

wind, 8